MAHATMA GANDHI

MAHATMA GANDHI

ODYSSEYS

LAURA K. MURRAY

CREATIVE EDUCATION · CREATIVE PAPERBACKS

Published by Creative Education and Creative Paperbacks
P.O. Box 227, Mankato, Minnesota 56002
Creative Education and Creative Paperbacks are imprints of
The Creative Company
www.thecreativecompany.us

Design by Blue Design (www.bluedes.com)
Production by Colin O'Dea
Art direction by Rita Marshall
Printed in the United States of America

Photographs by 123RF (Ajith Achuthan), Alamy (Dinodia
Photos, Dinodia Photos/Hulton Archive, Pictorial Press
Ltd, jeremy sutton-hibbert), Creative Commons Wikimedia
(Kanu Gandhi, Mohandas K. Gandhi/Dinodia Photo Library,
gandhiserve.org), The Design Lab, Getty Images (Bettmann,
Central Press/Stringer/Picture Post, Hulton Archive/Stringer,
Imagno/Hulton Archive, IndiaPictures/UIG, Douglas Miller/
Stringer/Hulton Archive, Universal History Archive/UIG,
Srividya Vanamamalai/EyeEm), iStockphoto (arismart, Joel
Carillet, Diy13, nilanewsom, rrodrickbeiler)

Library of Congress Cataloging-in-Publication Data
Names: Murray, Laura K., author.
Title: Mahatma Gandhi / Laura K. Murray.
Series: Odysseys in peace.
Includes bibliographical references and index.
Summary: A biography of Indian activist Mahatma Gandhi,
examining his position as a leader of nonviolent civil
disobedience, as well as his emphasis on fasting and other
social stances.
Identifiers: ISBN 978-1-64026-164-8 (hardcover) / ISBN
978-1-62832-727-4 (pbk) / ISBN 978-1-64000-282-1
(eBook)
This title has been submitted for CIP processing under LCCN
2019935251.

First Edition HC 9 8 7 6 5 4 3 2 1
First Edition PBK 9 8 7 6 5 4 3 2 1

CONTENTS

Introduction

On one side stood the mighty British Empire and its powerful military. On the other was a frail man with wire-rimmed glasses, clad in a traditional white-cotton *dhoti*. Behind him were thousands of peaceful protestors who were willing to be arrested—even killed—for their cause. That was the image Mahatma Gandhi conjured in the minds of people around the world as they watched India struggle for independence from Great Britain.

OPPOSITE: When an Indian army colonel once asked about his inspiration, Gandhi reportedly gave the colonel his glasses, noting that they provided him with "the vision to free India."

Gandhi's calls for political and social change first ignited the spirits of Indians living in South Africa and then those in India as well. Through acts of mass, nonviolent resistance, he demonstrated the power of peaceful protest to effect change as he looked to improve the lives of the disenfranchised.

Gandhi began his career as a shy lawyer. But his deeply held beliefs in justice and truth helped transform him into a renowned figure. As he developed his philosophies about truth, tolerance, and nonviolence, he garnered legions of dedicated adherents who wanted to follow his example of living simply, empowering others, and striving to unify all peoples. Although he continues to face criticism from various channels today, Mahatma Gandhi is known the world over as the standard bearer of nonviolent protest.

Birth of a Leader

Mohandas Karamchand Gandhi was born October 2, 1869, in the western Indian city of Porbandar. Nicknamed "Mohan," he grew up in an elite Hindu family as the youngest of four children. His father, Karamchand, held a high position in the regional government, while his mother, Putlibai, was a religious woman who fasted and went to temple regularly. Gandhi's family followed religious traditions of vegetarianism, fasting, tolerance, and

OPPOSITE: In South Africa, Gandhi was ordered to remove his turban while serving as a translator in a court case; he refused, left the courtroom, and wrote a letter of protest to the press.

nonviolence. At the time, India was a colony that had been controlled by the British Crown since 1858. Indians were considered British subjects.

When Gandhi was about 7 years old, his family moved more than 100 miles (161 km) northeast to the city of Rajkot. Gandhi was shy and, by his own admission, an unremarkable student. He was just 13 years old when he was married to a local girl named Kasturba through an arranged marriage. Later in his life, Gandhi spoke out against child marriage. He went through a period of teenage rebellion that included secretly eating meat and being inclined toward atheism.

As he grew up, Gandhi began developing his perspectives on tolerance and truth that would guide him throughout his life. Listening to his dying father's discussions with friends of other faiths, Gandhi was influenced to be tolerant of different religions. Gandhi also cultivated a belief in morality as the basis for all things and in truth as the substance for morality. "Truth became my sole objective," he later recalled. "It began to grow in magnitude every day, and my definition of it also has been ever widening." He also gravitated toward the idea of responding to evil with goodness.

Although Gandhi was interested in the medical field, his family wanted him to be a lawyer so that he could qualify for a position in the government. At 18 years old, Gandhi journeyed to London to study law at the Inner Temple (an inn, or college, of English law). His wife and newborn son remained in India. Gandhi's mother was nervous for her son to travel so far away but gave permission after he took an oath to avoid corrupt behavior. Leaders of Gandhi's caste forbade him from going abroad, but he ignored their order.

Gandhi's three years in London exposed him to many new ideas and people that shaped his views on religion, morality, and society. Through his involvement in London's Vegetarian Society, Gandhi met various British writers and thinkers whose beliefs included simple living, cooperation, and socialism. His new acquaintances introduced him to the Christian Bible and, perhaps most importantly, the Hindu Bhagavad Gita, which Gandhi later called his "spiritual dictionary." Gandhi's experiences in London further developed his philosophies about the unity of all peoples and religions.

n 1891, Gandhi returned to India to practice law but had little success. Plagued throughout his early life by stage fright and what he called his "constitutional shyness," Gandhi found it difficult to argue cases in court. He soon took the opportunity to move alone to South Africa as a legal adviser for an Indian trading company. In 1893, Gandhi arrived in the city of Durban on the east coast of South Africa. No one, including

Gandhi himself, could have predicted that the move to South Africa would forge his future path as a renowned leader for civil and human rights rather than a lawyer.

Gandhi was posted in the British colony of Natal. At the time, South Africa was divided into two British colonies and two Dutch colonies. The minority Indian population—which consisted mainly of traders and indentured workers—was struggling for representative rights and equal treatment. Despite being British subjects, Indians endured discrimination and prejudice of varying degrees in the colonies. Some Indians did not have voting or property rights, while others were segregated from white citizens, forced to pay unfair taxes, or subjected to other forms of discrimination.

Soon after his arrival, Gandhi experienced a series of injustices firsthand, including being thrown out of

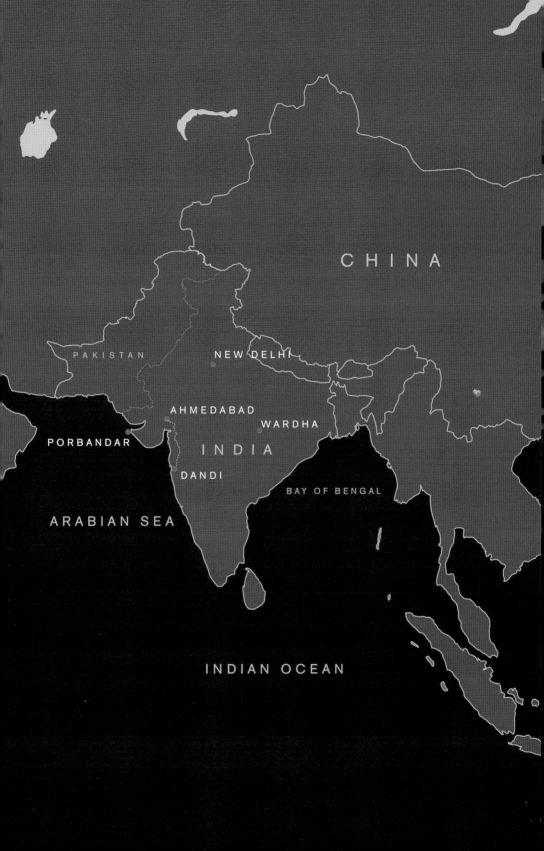

a first-class train car despite his first-class ticket. In his autobiography, Gandhi recalled deciding what he should do next. "The hardship to which I was subjected was superficial—only a symptom of the deep disease of color prejudice," he wrote. So he decided to "root out the disease and suffer hardships in the process."

The unfair treatment served as a turning point in Gandhi's life. Until then, he had not been particularly interested in political activism. Now, however, he felt called to fight injustice, and he realized his potential role in mobilizing the Indian community to action. Over the next two decades, Gandhi used his legal background to guide his work, meeting with politicians, writing to newspapers, opposing unfair laws, and organizing petitions. He soon became a spokesperson for Indian rights and overcame his shyness in front of crowds. In 1894, along with other Indian activists, Gandhi established the Natal Indian Congress, an organization dedicated to fighting discrimination and empowering Indians. Many Indians in South Africa found their champion in Gandhi and threw their support behind him.

Gandhi's work also earned him vicious opponents. In 1897, upon returning to Natal after bringing his wife and two of their children from India, he was met by a mob. The white, European crowd was upset at a widely circulated pamphlet he had written against the treatment of Indians. They attacked him with stones, bricks, and eggs, beating him until the police superintendent's wife, who was passing by, positioned herself between Gandhi and the angry crowd as police were summoned. The police later disguised Gandhi as a constable so he could escape the area unnoticed. Gandhi declined to press charges.

Gandhi was finding that traditional tactics were not leading to the social change he and his followers urgently sought.

Meanwhile, Gandhi continued his spiritual studies. He read the Quran, Hindu scriptures, philosophy books, and Christian writings. He decided that all religions were true and imperfect. He became interested in leading a life marked by simplicity and the rejection of material goods. As he gained followers interested in his teachings, he established two community settlements dedicated to simple living. He also launched the newspaper the *Indian Opinion* to give voice to the Indian community in South Africa.

Gandhi wanted to demonstrate to the British that Indians deserved equal treatment as respectable and loyal

British subjects. During the Second Boer War, Gandhi coordinated the Natal Indian Ambulance Corps of stretcher-bearers. Approximately 1,100 Indians served in the Corps in support of the British, who declared victory in 1902. Much to Gandhi's distress, it was soon clear that the Indians' war service would not result in their improved treatment under the British government.

Gandhi was finding that traditional tactics were not leading to the social change he and his followers urgently sought. He began developing a technique of nonviolent resistance. He called his concept *satyagraha*. Variously translated as "truth force," "soul force," or "firmness in truth," satyagraha involved breaking unreasonable or unfair laws and being open to suffering punishment. Satyagraha resulted in the suffering of the self rather than of an opponent. It also involved actions of peaceful

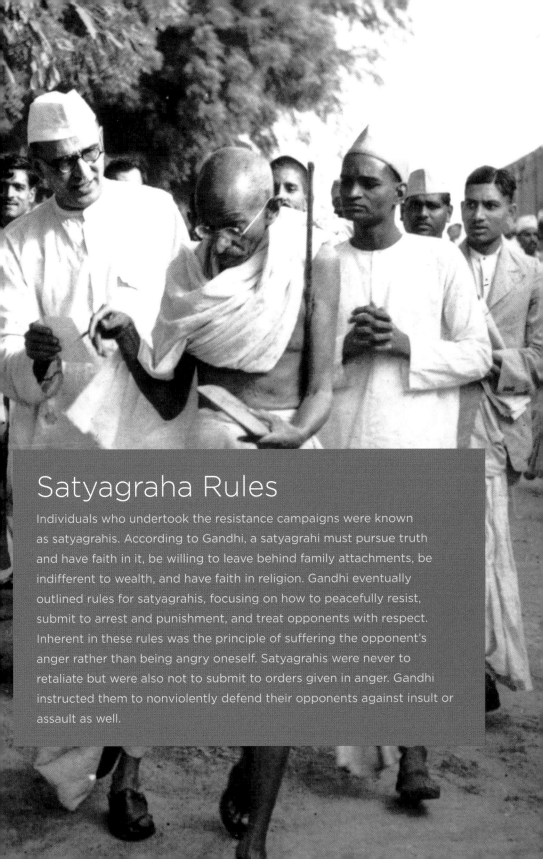

Satyagraha Rules

Individuals who undertook the resistance campaigns were known as satyagrahis. According to Gandhi, a satyagrahi must pursue truth and have faith in it, be willing to leave behind family attachments, be indifferent to wealth, and have faith in religion. Gandhi eventually outlined rules for satyagrahis, focusing on how to peacefully resist, submit to arrest and punishment, and treat opponents with respect. Inherent in these rules was the principle of suffering the opponent's anger rather than being angry oneself. Satyagrahis were never to retaliate but were also not to submit to orders given in anger. Gandhi instructed them to nonviolently defend their opponents against insult or assault as well.

noncooperation, such as boycotts and protests.

Gandhi's philosophy centered on the search for truth, or *satya*. Gandhi believed that truth could be attained only through *ahimsa*, nonviolence toward all living things. In Gandhi's view, this nonviolent resistance would allow each side to see the other's humanity. "Satyagraha is essentially the weapon of the truthful," he said, calling it "more potent than physical strength, which is as worthless as straw when compared with the former." Gandhi viewed nonviolent resistance as a matter of principle and as more than simply a means to reform. The use of satyagraha would become a hallmark of Gandhi's lasting legacy.

"Truth is like a vast tree, which yields more and more fruit, the more you nurture it."

- Mahatma Gandhi, autobiography

Launching the Resistance

Gandhi soon organized his first satyagraha campaign to protest injustice in South Africa. In 1906, a new law known as the "Black Act" required Indians in the Transvaal colony to be registered and fingerprinted. Gandhi called on Indians to peacefully disobey the law and accept punishment. "Indians in the Transvaal will stagger humanity without shedding a single drop of

OPPOSITE: Though Gandhi's beliefs were largely shaped by his time in London, his years in Africa are what led to his political activism and to his becoming known as a visionary civil rights leader.

29

blood," he wrote.

In 1908, Gandhi was arrested and found guilty of having no registration certificate. Refusing to obey the order to leave the colony, he and other leaders were imprisoned for two months. "Our success in bringing this campaign to this stage is a triumph for truth," he wrote before being jailed. It was the first of many times Gandhi would be arrested during his lifetime. More than 2,000 people joined in demonstrations against the Black Act, including burning their registration permits. The law was repealed in 1911.

In March 1913, the satyagraha campaign found a new cause when the government refused to recognize Hindu and Muslim marriages. This injustice resulted in Indian women joining the nonviolent resistance. A few months later, a new campaign began as Gandhi rallied supporters to protest a tax on formerly indentured Indian workers. He called on miners and others to march to the border of the Natal and Transvaal colonies and cross illegally. "May the community have the strength and the faith to go through the fire!" he said. More than 2,000 people, including men, women, and children, joined the march and crossed the border. Gandhi was arrested, released on bail, and re-arrested twice when he rejoined the protests, which swept through other towns. Peaceful strikers were imprisoned, beaten, and even killed, causing widespread public outcry.

In 1914, Gandhi agreed to end the satyagraha campaign as the government ended the tax, recognized the Indian marriages, and pardoned the resisters. Indians in South Africa continued to face other oppressive laws and discrimination. Still, Gandhi saw the agreement as proof

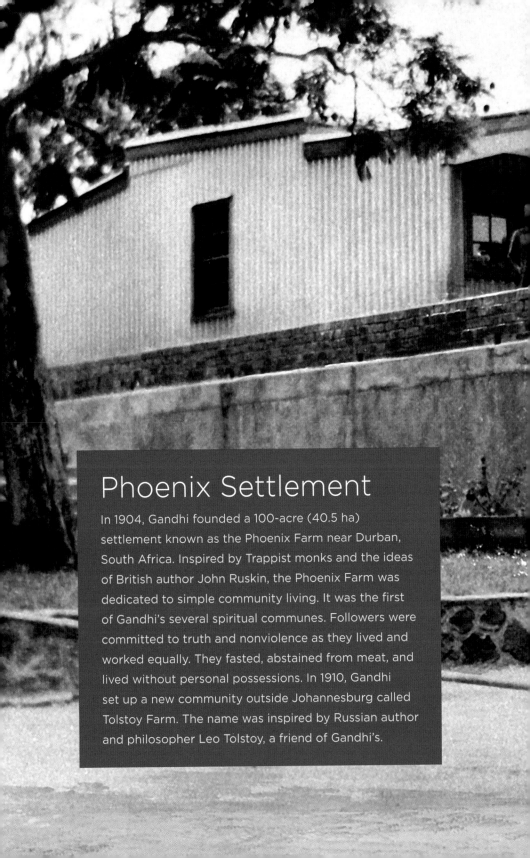

Phoenix Settlement

In 1904, Gandhi founded a 100-acre (40.5 ha) settlement known as the Phoenix Farm near Durban, South Africa. Inspired by Trappist monks and the ideas of British author John Ruskin, the Phoenix Farm was dedicated to simple community living. It was the first of Gandhi's several spiritual communes. Followers were committed to truth and nonviolence as they lived and worked equally. They fasted, abstained from meat, and lived without personal possessions. In 1910, Gandhi set up a new community outside Johannesburg called Tolstoy Farm. The name was inspired by Russian author and philosopher Leo Tolstoy, a friend of Gandhi's.

of the power of nonviolent resistance against injustice.

By this time, Gandhi was becoming widely recognized. He soon earned the name by which he would be known to the world: Mahatma, meaning "great soul" in Sanskrit. When Gandhi decided to return to his homeland of India, British and Afrikaner leaders in South Africa were not disappointed to see the agitator leave. "The Saint has left our shores," General Jan Smuts wrote to a friend, "I sincerely hope forever."

In January 1915, Gandhi returned to India transformed from the inside out. When he had left for South Africa more than 20 years earlier, he had dressed in a suit and tie. He was shy and shrank from public speaking. Now, though, he wore simple clothing of a dhoti and shawl and was welcomed as a hero. His time in South Africa had helped him refine his philosophies and given him experience in leading people in nonviolent resistance against oppression. He was prepared to fight for truth and justice while continuing to develop nonviolent strategies. His life was now dedicated to simplicity, prayer, fasting, and meditation. His views on British rule were changing as well.

Gandhi spent a year traveling throughout India with his wife to gain an understanding of conditions across the country. Riding in a third-class train compartment, he was shocked at the poverty and

Peace Prize-less

Although Gandhi received many accolades throughout his life, there is one that, perhaps surprisingly, he never won: the Nobel Peace Prize. The subject has come up so often that the Nobel Prize website includes an article dedicated to it, referencing Gandhi as "the Missing Laureate." Gandhi was nominated for the prize five times. Criticisms throughout the years included negative views of his political leadership and his perceived dedication to Indian nationalism over universal peace. In 1948, the committee did not award a prize, citing "no suitable living candidate." The article states that it is "reasonable to assume" that Gandhi would have won the award that year.

NOBELS FREDSSENTER • NOBEL PEACE CENTER

YN • BROADMINDEDNESS   HÅP • HOPE   ENGASJEMENT corruption that pervaded Indian society. Vowing to improve the people's conditions, he engaged in local movements and helped campaign for workers' rights. He established a communal settlement, called Satyagraha Ashram, in the northwestern city of Ahmedabad. The community was open to women and men of all backgrounds, religions, and castes, even those considered untouchables (the lowest of the caste system).

In 1919, the British established the Rowlatt Acts, which gave the government the power to imprison without trial those suspected of sedition. Gandhi called the bills "instruments of oppression," seeing them as an affront to Indian civil rights. They became known as India's Black Acts. Gandhi called for a satyagraha campaign and quickly condemned the violence that broke out upon his arrest. "If we cannot conduct this movement without the slightest violence on our side, the movement might have to be abandoned," he said. However, tensions soon spiraled into bloodshed when British Indian Army troops killed nearly 400 unarmed protesters in a city park in what became known as the Jallianwala Bagh (Amritsar) Massacre. More than 1,200 were wounded. Despite Gandhi's previous support for British rule, the massacre convinced him that India needed to gain full independence.

Leading the Indian National Congress, he began organizing a satyagraha campaign against the British government, focusing on freeing India from Britain's economic control. He encouraged Indian citizens to purchase locally made goods rather than those imported from Britain. He also called for boycotts of British goods as well as government offices and schools. Thousands

British Indian Army troops killed nearly 400 unarmed protesters.

of people joined the campaign. However, incidents of violence, including the attack of a police station by demonstrators, caused Gandhi to end the satyagraha in 1922.

In March 1922, Gandhi was arrested and faced trial for conspiring against the British government in what became known as the Great Trial. He pled guilty. In a statement, he explained that violent noncooperation would compound evil and that peaceful noncooperation would result in punishment. "I am here, therefore, to invite and submit cheerfully to the highest penalty that can be inflicted upon me for what in law is deliberate crime, and what appears to me to be the highest duty of a citizen," he said. He was sentenced to six years in prison but continued his activism from his cell.

Civil Disobedience

Gandhi's ideas of nonviolent resistance were influenced by the writings of American philosopher Henry David Thoreau. First published in 1849, Thoreau's essay "Civil Disobedience" argued that citizens should not put the law ahead of their consciences. According to Thoreau, if a law "is of such a nature that it requires you to be the agent of injustice to another, then, I say, break the law." Thoreau wrote the essay after being jailed in Massachusetts for not paying a poll tax in protest of slavery and the Mexican-American War. Later, American civil rights leaders, including **Martin Luther King Jr.**, were inspired by Thoreau's ideas.

OPPOSITE Gandhi wore traditional Indian clothing to the Round Table Conference in London in 1931, standing in stark contrast to the Western suits of the other men at the talks.

When riots between Hindus and Muslims broke out in 1924, he held a 21-day fast. Gandhi was released early due to illness.

In January 1930, the Indian National Congress officially called for independence from Britain. The organization's Indian Declaration of Independence stated, "The British Government in India has not only deprived the Indian people of their freedom but has based itself on the exploitation of the masses, and has ruined India economically, politically, culturally, and spiritually. We believe, therefore, that India must sever the British connection and attain *Purna Swaraj*, or complete independence." The Congress looked to Gandhi to lead a satyagraha campaign to win India's independence and change the course of the country's future.

"A life of sacrifice is the pinnacle of art and is full of true joy. Such life is the source of ever fresh springs of joy which never dry up and never satiate. *Yajna* [sacrifice] is not yajna if one feels it to be burdensome or annoying. Self-indulgence leads to destruction and renunciation to immortality. Joy has no independent existence. It depends upon our attitude to life."

- Mahatma Gandhi, letter to his nephew, 1930

Do or Die

Leading the fight for India's independence, Gandhi first focused the satyagraha campaign on the British monopoly on salt. Indians were not allowed to produce or sell their own salt. Instead, they were required to purchase costly, heavily taxed salt from the British. In 1930, Gandhi and a group of his followers began walking from his ashram to the Arabian Sea to protest the salt tax. As they marched more than 200 miles (322 km) over a

OPPOSITE: Before setting out on the Salt March, Gandhi wrote to the British Empire's representative in India and volunteered to suspend the march if the salt tax were repealed, but the representative never responded.

span of 24 days, crowds flocked to listen to Gandhi's speeches. Many joined the march. When the group arrived at the sea, they illegally collected salt from the shore in a symbolic act. The Salt March inspired thousands of Indians to commit acts of civil disobedience. Over the next two months, Gandhi and more than 60,000 others were arrested and jailed, and many were beaten by police. Gandhi's arrest prompted even more people to join the peaceful demonstrations. The marches also attracted the world's attention, and Gandhi was named *TIME* magazine's 1930 "Man of the Year."

Gandhi called off the campaign and was released from prison in 1931. That same year, he attended the London Round Table Conference as a representative of the Indian National Congress. The conference was a disappointment, as Britain refused to grant independence,

Gandhi was named *TIME* magazine's 1930 "Man of the Year."

and India's religious leaders were not unified. Gandhi was imprisoned yet again upon his return to India, and British officials attempted to stifle his influence. In 1932, he began a fast "until death" from his prison cell to protest a decision to give the untouchable caste separate political representation. "This is a god-given opportunity that has come to me to offer my life as a final sacrifice to the downtrodden," he said. The massive public response resulted in a negotiation to reverse the decision, ending Gandhi's fast after six days.

In 1934, Gandhi announced his retirement from politics. He and his followers set up a new ashram in central India called *Sevagram* ("Village of Service"). He traveled throughout the country for the next few years,

As at Wardha
C.P.
India.
23.7.'39.

Dear friend,

Friends have been urging me to write to you for the sake of humanity. But I nave resisted their request, because of the feeling that any letter from me would be an impertinence. Something tells me that I must not calculate and that I must make my appeal for whatever it may be worth.

It is quite clear that you are today the one person in the world who can prevent a war which may reduce humanity to the savage state. Must you pay that price for an object however worthy it may appear to you to be ? Will you listen to the appeal of one who has seliberately shunned the method of war not without considerable success? Any way I anticipate your forgiveneas, if I have erred in writing to you.

Herr Hitler
Berlin
Germany.

I remain,

Your sincere friend

M.K.Gandhi

48

visiting villages and advocating for better treatment, conditions, and education. The dawning of World War II (1939–1945) spurred Gandhi to return to political life and embark on another satyagraha campaign.

Gandhi wrote twice to Adolf Hitler, urging peace. "It is quite clear that you are today the one person in the world who can prevent a war which may reduce humanity to the savage state," Gandhi wrote just before Germany invaded Poland. It is unknown if Hitler read the letters. When Great Britain declared

Spinning-Wheel Symbolism

The traditional spinning wheel, or *charkha*, became a popular illustration of Gandhi's teachings on nonviolent protest. Rejecting British imported cloth, Gandhi used the spinning wheel as a symbol of India's economic independence as he called for boycotts of British goods. It also served as a practical means of living when Gandhi encouraged citizens to be self-sufficient in making their own cloth. Gandhi called on his followers to spin daily and viewed the spinning wheel as a symbol of love of humankind. However, the boycotts led to violence when crowds began burning imported goods.

war on Germany, India was forced to provide soldiers, food, and other resources. The British did not include any elected Indian leaders in this decision and censored criticism. The Indian National Congress declared to British officials that they would support the war only if it resulted in Indian independence. In response, Britain threatened to empower India's Muslim League instead. Still, Indian leaders did not plan to give up the fight for independence. Gandhi launched individual satyagraha campaigns, recruiting citizens to defy the censorship laws and speak out against the British. Many of the participants were arrested.

In 1942, Gandhi led a new movement, demanding that Britain "quit India." He told the Indian National Congress: "We shall either free India or die in the attempt; we shall not live to see the perpetuation of our slavery." He introduced a mantra for the campaign: "Do or die." The Congress passed a "Quit India Resolution" that declared India's independence. The night before Gandhi was to make a public speech, he, Kasturba, and most members of the Congress were imprisoned. The British prohibited press reports on the resolution.

Even with Gandhi and the leaders in prison, the movement forged ahead—surprisingly, assisted in part by the British. In an effort to explain the arrests and paint the Indian leaders negatively, British officials described

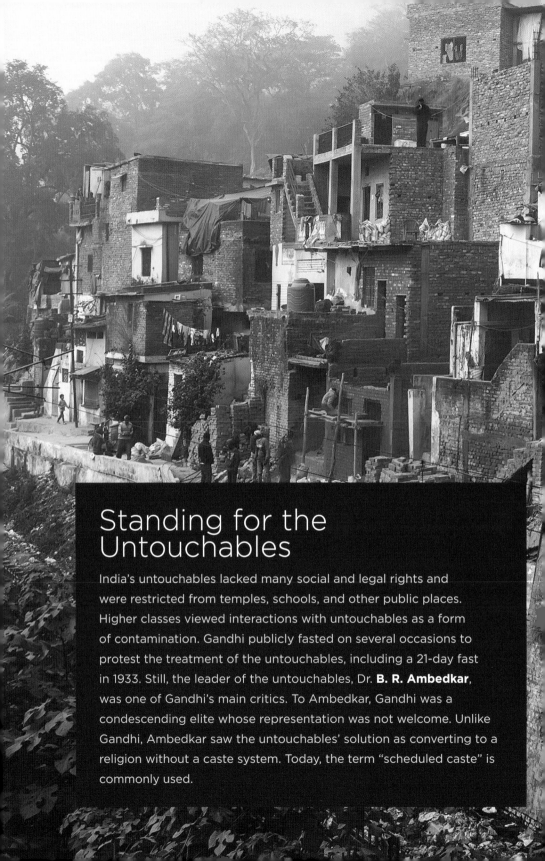

Standing for the Untouchables

India's untouchables lacked many social and legal rights and were restricted from temples, schools, and other public places. Higher classes viewed interactions with untouchables as a form of contamination. Gandhi publicly fasted on several occasions to protest the treatment of the untouchables, including a 21-day fast in 1933. Still, the leader of the untouchables, Dr. **B. R. Ambedkar**, was one of Gandhi's main critics. To Ambedkar, Gandhi was a condescending elite whose representation was not welcome. Unlike Gandhi, Ambedkar saw the untouchables' solution as converting to a religion without a caste system. Today, the term "scheduled caste" is commonly used.

thwarted plans for strikes and various attacks against the British government. The officials concluded, "The success of the proposed campaign would paralyze not only the ordinary civil administration of India, but her whole war effort." To the surprise of the British, Indian citizens used the description as a plan for rebellion. They rioted, attacked railways, cut telephone wires, and burned down police stations. "The chief irony of 1942 in India was that the awesome power of the press to inspire united action was unleashed by the British government," writes historian Paul Greenough. More than 100,000 were arrested, while approximately 1,000 were killed. Gandhi was distraught that "Quit India" had devolved into violent conflict. But peaceful strikes and protests also continued.

In February 1943, after a week of silent prayer, an

already ill Gandhi went on a public fast in his prison cell. For 21 days, he took only citrus juice added to water. The fast made him so weak that officials braced themselves for his death, but he lived. Kasturba died in prison in 1944. Gandhi was released a few months later.

n 1945, Britain's newly elected Labour Party leaders began negotiating for Indian independence. Meanwhile, tensions escalated between India's Hindus and Muslims. Both the Indian National Congress and the Muslim League were concerned about their role and power within a new government. In 1946, widespread riots broke out between Hindus and Muslims in the city of Calcutta (present-day Kolkata). When a Muslim leader declared August 16 as "Direct Action Day," events spun out of control and into bloody violence.

On August 15, 1947, after nearly 90 years of British colonial rule, India declared its independence from Great Britain. However, the outcome was not what Gandhi had campaigned for. Instead of a unified India that embraced all religions, two independent states of India and Pakistan were formed, divided by religion. India was largely Hindu, while Pakistan was predominantly Muslim. The country's partition, or division, resulted in one of the largest mass migrations in history, as more than 10 million people relocated. Conflict exploded and ended in mass casualties. In September, Gandhi's fasting put a stop to rioting in Calcutta.

OPPOSITE After an eight-month trial, Gandhi's assassin and an accomplice were sentenced to death; six other men found complicit in the crime were sentenced to life in prison.

Gandhi turned his attention to bridging the divisions between Hindus and Muslims. He supported Muslims living in India and began to fast for peace. He ended the fast when community leaders pledged they would live in peace and that Muslim rights would be protected.

Gandhi's calls for religious tolerance made him enemies on both sides. On January 30, 1948, Gandhi was assassinated while walking to a prayer meeting in the city of New Delhi. Upset at Gandhi's tolerance of Muslims, a young Hindu extremist stepped out of the crowd and shot Gandhi three times from close range, killing him. Mahatma Gandhi was 78 years old. The extremist and his accomplices had made another attempt on Gandhi's life just 10 days before.

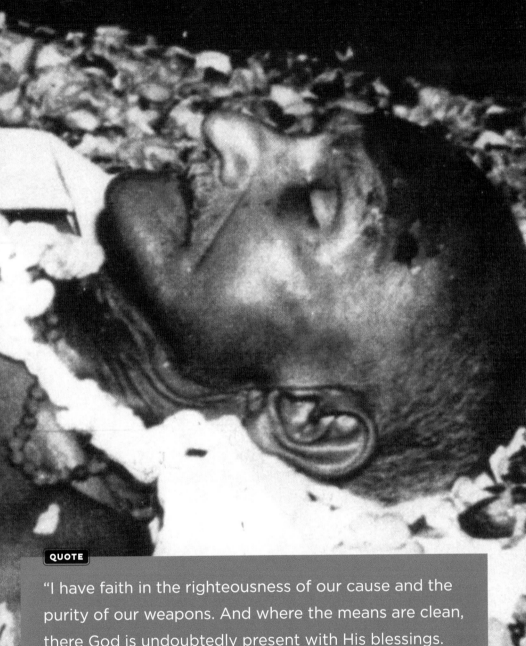

"I have faith in the righteousness of our cause and the purity of our weapons. And where the means are clean, there God is undoubtedly present with His blessings. And where these three combine, there defeat is an impossibility." — **Mahatma Gandhi, before the Salt March, 1932**

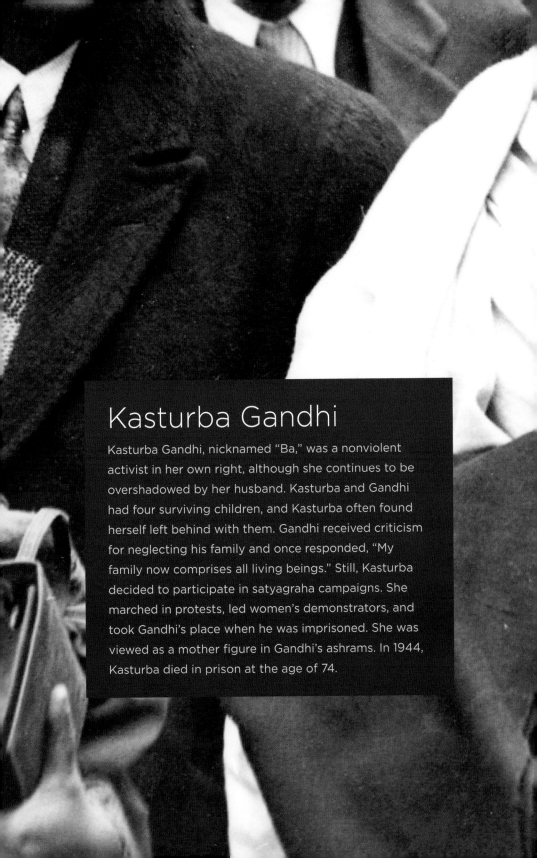

Kasturba Gandhi

Kasturba Gandhi, nicknamed "Ba," was a nonviolent activist in her own right, although she continues to be overshadowed by her husband. Kasturba and Gandhi had four surviving children, and Kasturba often found herself left behind with them. Gandhi received criticism for neglecting his family and once responded, "My family now comprises all living beings." Still, Kasturba decided to participate in satyagraha campaigns. She marched in protests, led women's demonstrators, and took Gandhi's place when he was imprisoned. She was viewed as a mother figure in Gandhi's ashrams. In 1944, Kasturba died in prison at the age of 74.

Criticism and Legacy

People in India and around the world mourned Gandhi's death. "The light has gone out of our lives, and there is darkness everywhere," said India's prime minister Jawaharlal Nehru in a radio address. "For the light that shone in this country was no ordinary light. [It] … will illumine this country for many more years, and a thousand years later, that light will be seen in this country, and the world will see it,

OPPOSITE: Mourned the world over, Gandhi was cremated along one of India's sacred rivers within 24 hours of his death, in accordance with ancient Hindu tradition.

and it will give solace to innumerable hearts."

Nearly one million people joined the funeral procession. Riots broke out in some areas, while celebrations by extremist groups occurred elsewhere. Gandhi's ashes were sent throughout India and scattered off the South African coast. A memorial called Raj Ghat was erected to mark the place of his cremation. Located in Delhi, Raj Ghat is a black metal platform near the Yamuna River. At one end of the platform, a flame is kept burning.

Gandhi had many critics during his life, sometimes from opposing sides of a single issue. Some viewed him as a self-righteous leader. Others questioned his commitment to universal pacifism or criticized him for focusing on other initiatives besides India's independence. Others took issue with his involvement with the untouchables or his refusal to call for the elimination of India's caste system altogether.

Still, many of Gandhi's critics admitted their admiration of his steadfast principles of nonviolence. Even Jan Smuts, who had been relieved at Gandhi's departure from South Africa, later said he held no ill feelings toward the man. Smuts remarked that it had been his "fate to be the antagonist of a man for whom even then I had the highest respect."

Gandhi continues to be alternately praised and criticized in present-day examinations. Some critiques are based on his perceived self-righteousness or his rejection of technology and industry. Other disapprovals stem from how Gandhi treated his wife and his belief in traditional gender roles regarding men's and women's places in society. (Although he did not comment directly on this, his behavior seemed to indicate that he believed women should be the primary caregivers at home.) Gandhi's defenders assert that he was ahead of his time in many ways and credit him for welcoming women's participation in the resistance campaigns and recognizing their leadership capabilities.

Scholar Vinay Lal points out that much of the criticism lies in Gandhi's ambiguity. Lal points to followers who discovered that "Gandhi was a better Christian than many who call themselves Christian." Gandhi rejected certain religious teachings that he disagreed with, such as those that degraded certain groups. He also did not conform to all traditional practices. Unlike other Hindus, he did not feel the need to visit temples. Therefore, some Hindus felt as though Gandhi was acting as a false representative of their community. Others did not appreciate his criticism of sacred texts.

In Africa, particularly, Gandhi has a controversial legacy. When a statue was unveiled at the University of Ghana in 2016, protests erupted, and more than 1,000 people signed a petition to remove it. Demonstrators called Gandhi racist, pointing to his statements asserting that black Africans were inferior to Indians. They called for representation of African figures instead. The university agreed to remove the statue. "While acknowledging that, human as he was, Mahatma Gandhi may have had his flaws, we must remember that people evolve," said the university in a statement.

Much of the work Gandhi began, such as the improvement of conditions for all Indian groups, remains to be completed. Gandhi was not able to sustain lasting unity between Hindus and Muslims, and tensions between India and Pakistan have escalated into modern wars

To Stage, Screen, and Beyond

Since his death, Gandhi has inspired the creation of books, music, plays, comics, and films, with some of them taking a critical view of him. In 1979, Gandhi was the inspiration behind the opera *Satyagraha* by American composer Philip Glass. In 1982, Gandhi's life was depicted in the British-Indian film *Gandhi*. It starred British actor Ben Kingsley in the title role. The 3-hour epic was nominated for 11 Academy Awards and won 8 at the 1983 ceremony, including Best Picture, Best Director (Richard Attenborough), and Best Actor (Kingsley).

and ongoing hostilities. Criticism has grown louder from Hindu nationalists who believe his tolerance of Muslims led to deeper divisions within India.

One of Gandhi's indisputable legacies is his inspiration to activists who have led successful nonviolent resistance movements around the world. Leaders include Nelson Mandela, who worked to end apartheid in South Africa through both peaceful and violent means, and Martin Luther King Jr., who struggled to achieve equal rights for all races in the United States through nonviolent resistance. "To other countries I may go as a tourist, but to India I go as a pilgrim," King said while visiting India in 1959, referring to his reverence for Gandhi's work. Gandhi's methods of resistance have continued to prompt academic studies and serve as guides for all manner of conflict resolution.

Present-day Britain has been quick to recognize Gandhi's legacy. In 2015, Gandhi became the first Indian to be represented in London's Parliament Square when a statue was erected in his honor. Jill McGivering of BBC News points out, "There is some irony in the fact that even as Gandhi is being so warmly embraced by the British establishment that once mocked him, his legacy in India is more ambivalent." Gandhi's grandson, Arun Gandhi, believed that Gandhi would not have desired such accolades. "My grandfather didn't want people to erect statues," he said. "He wanted people to follow his message."

Since Gandhi's death, he has remained a renowned figurehead of both peaceful protest and India's movement for independence. He has become known to many as the Father of India, with his image on postage stamps and in public buildings. Historians debate the importance of the role that his "Quit India" campaign played in securing India's independence. Still, many consider it to be a critical part of the struggle. His birthday, October 2, is an Indian national holiday called "Gandhi Jayanti." People celebrate with prayer services, ceremonies, art exhibitions, and awards for initiatives promoting nonviolence. In 2007, the United Nations declared October 2 as the International Day of Nonviolence.

According to Gandhi biographer Judith M. Brown,

"Fundamentally, he was a man of vision and action, who asked many of the profoundest questions that face humankind as it struggles to live in community.... As a man of his time, he became a man for all times and all places." Albeit imperfect, his concept of nonviolent resistance demonstrated a radical new strategy for enacting social change. It has ignited campaigns around the world and spurred other leaders to oppose injustice through peaceful means. Gandhi's messages of truth, love, and tolerance continue to resonate with all those who struggle in a broken and fearful world to mend relationships and seek justice.

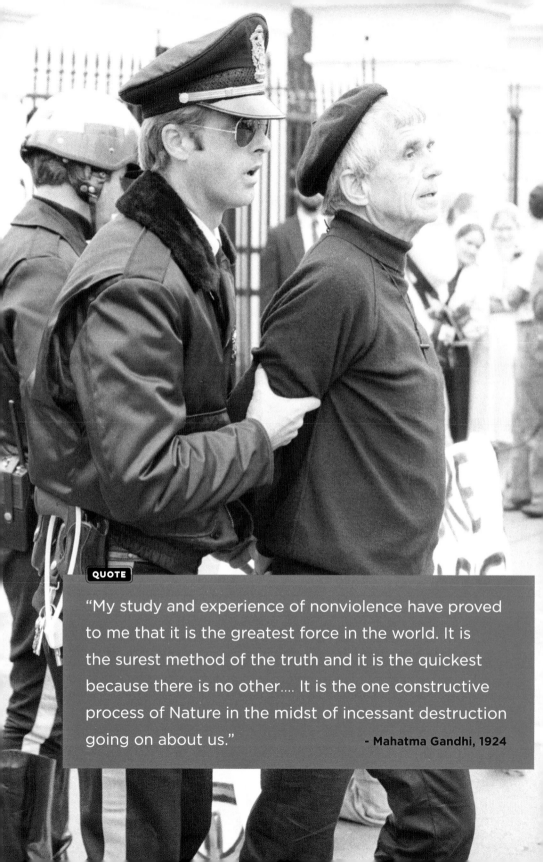

"My study and experience of nonviolence have proved to me that it is the greatest force in the world. It is the surest method of the truth and it is the quickest because there is no other.... It is the one constructive process of Nature in the midst of incessant destruction going on about us."

— Mahatma Gandhi, 1924

Timeline

1869   Mohandas Karamchand Gandhi is born in Porbandar, India, on October 2.

1888   In September, Gandhi arrives in London to study law and is exposed to many new ideas. He returns to India in 1891 after completing his studies.

1893   Gandhi arrives in Durban, South Africa, and soon becomes the spokesperson for the Indian minority.

1894   Gandhi helps establish the Natal Indian Congress.

1899   Gandhi organizes the Natal Indian Ambulance Corps in support of Britain during the Second Boer War.

1906   Gandhi organizes his first satyagraha campaign in protest of a law requiring the registration of Indians in the South African Transvaal colony.

1915   Gandhi returns to India in January and focuses his attention on improving conditions for Indians.

1919   In April, Gandhi organizes a satyagraha in response to the Rowlatt Acts.

1922   Gandhi is arrested for sedition and pleads guilty during the "Great Trial." He is sentenced to six years in jail but is released early.

1930   Gandhi leads supporters on the Salt March to the Arabian Sea to protest the British tax on salt.

1932   Gandhi vows to fast until death to protest an unfair law regarding India's untouchable caste. He ends the fast after six days when the law is reversed.

1942   Gandhi launches the "Quit India" movement calling for India's independence.

1947   India gains independence from Britain on August 15, and is separated into India and Pakistan. Gandhi calls for religious tolerance between Hindus and Muslims.

1948   On January 30, Gandhi is assassinated in New Delhi at the age of 78.

Selected Bibliography

Boissoneault, Lorraine. "The Speech That Brought India to the Brink of Independence." *Smithsonian.* August 8, 2017. https://www.smithsonianmag.com/history/speech-brought -india-brink-independence-180964366/.

Desai, Anita. "A Different Gandhi." *The New York Review of Books.* April 28, 2011. http://www.nybooks.com /articles/2011/04/28/different-gandhi/.

Gandhi, Mahatma. *An Autobiography: The Story of My Experiments with Truth.* Boston: Beacon Press, 1993.

———. *The Essential Writings.* New York: Oxford University, 2008.

Hardiman, David. "Gandhi: Reckless Teenager to Father of India." *BBC.* http://www.bbc.co.uk/timelines/zpdqmp3.

Lal, Vinay. "The Gandhi Everyone Loves to Hate." *Economic & Political Weekly.* October 4, 2008. https://www.epw.in /journal/2008/40/special-articles/gandhi-everyone-loves -hate.html.

"Mohandas K. Gandhi: The Indian Leader at Home and Abroad." *New York Times.* January 31, 1948. https://archive .nytimes.com/www.nytimes.com/learning /general/onthisday/bday/1002.html.

Tønnesson, Øyvind. "Mahatma Gandhi, the Missing Laureate." *NobelPrize.org*. December 1, 1999. https://www.nobelprize .org/nobel_prizes/themes/peace/gandhi/?utm _content=gandhi_text.

Wolpert, Stanley. *Gandhi's Passion: The Life and Legacy of Mahatma Gandhi*. New York: Oxford University, 2001.

Endnotes

Adolf Hitler	(1889–1945)—dictator and leader of the German Nazi party; chancellor of Germany from 1933 to 1945
apartheid	South African system of laws that enforced segregation based on race
atheism	disbelief in the existence of God or gods
B. R. Ambedkar	(1891–1956)—an Indian activist and politician considered a founding father of the Republic of India; born to the "untouchables" caste, he worked to fight discrimination and later converted to Buddhism
Bhagavad Gita	an important Hindu scripture that is part of the Sanskrit epic poem the *Mahabharata*
boycotts	forms of protest involving refusals to purchase or use certain goods or withdrawals from commercial or social relationships
caste	a social class into which one is born; the Hindu caste system was based on the purest people (priests) being at the top

dhoti	a traditional Indian garment for men that is wrapped around the waist
disenfranchised	deprived of power or rights
imported	describing goods that are brought in from another country
indentured	bound to work for someone for a given amount of time
Indian National Congress	an Indian political party founded in 1885
Martin Luther King Jr.	(1929–68)—American minister and activist who became one of the most famous spokespersons of the civil rights movement from the 1950s until his death
meditation	the act of concentrated focus or contemplation
minority	a group that differs from the larger group, or majority
morality	beliefs about what is right and wrong
Muslim League	Indian political group founded in 1906 that advocated for a separate Muslim state; it was dissolved with the partition of India in 1947 and the creation of Pakistan
Nelson Mandela	(1918–2013)—South African lawyer and politician who led an antiapartheid campaign; after spending 27 years in jail, he served as president of South Africa from 1994 to 1999

Second Boer War	(1899–1902)—a conflict between the British Empire and the two Boer states, the South African Republic (Transvaal) and the Orange Free State, ending in British victory
sedition	an act intended to overthrow or destroy an authority
segregated	intentionally separated along racial, sexual, or religious lines
socialism	a practice based on the economic and political idea that everyone in a society owns and controls goods and services

Websites

Gandhi Research Foundation
http://www.gandhifoundation.net/

Conduct a virtual visit to India's Gandhi Research Foundation, including the Gandhi Museum.

Mahatma Gandhi
https://www.mkgandhi.org/

Explore some of Gandhi's works as well as others' writings about him.

Note: Every effort has been made to ensure that any websites listed above were active at the time of publication. However, because of the nature of the Internet, it is impossible to guarantee that these sites will remain active indefinitely or that their contents will not be altered.

Index